GUIDE TO FIGHTING SHIPS

Andrew Kershaw

Illustrated by Cliff and Wendy Meadway

Edited by Bill Bruce

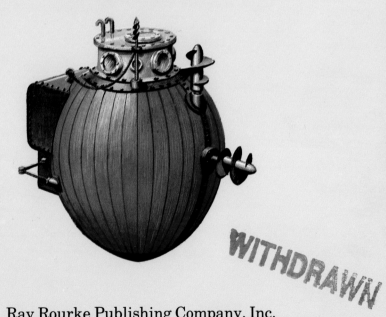

Ray Rourke Publishing Company, Inc.
Windermere, Florida 32786

Published by Ray Rourke Publishing Company, Inc.,
Windermere, Florida 32786.
Copyright © 1980 Piper Books Ltd.
Copyright © 1981 Ray Rourke Publishing Company, Inc.

Library of Congress Cataloging in Publication Data

Kershaw, Andrew.
  Guide to fighting ships.

  (Explorer guides)
  Includes index.
  SUMMARY: Traces the development of fighting ships
from the war galleys launched by the Greeks and
Persians to those used today.
  1. Warships—History—Juvenile literature.
[1. Warships—History]   I. Meadway, Clifford.
II. Meadway, Wendy.   III. Bruce, Bill.   IV. Title.
V750.K47   1981   359.8'3
ISBN 0-86592-016-8   AACR2
                                          81-525

Below: A modern naval frigate,
fast moving and packed with
many modern electronic
devices and powerful weapons.

Contents

About This Book

Ships have been used in war since the days when skin-clad men and women on floating logs threw stones at each other. Today, the world of fighting ships has entered the realms of high technology. Missiles, supersonic aircraft, computers and deep-diving submarines are all part of the modern naval scene. In between, there were the galleys rowed by sweating slaves, Norsemen in their longships, the mighty galleons of Spain and the period when the battleship ruled the sea. The story of fighting ships is rich in history and adventure. This book combines the flavor of that history with information to give the past a basis in fact.

The First Warships

The earliest purpose built fighting ships were war galleys launched by the Greeks and Persians during the 6th century BC. War galleys were propelled by oars rather than sails – this not only increased their power but also made steering easier. Less than a century later, the first great sea battle of ancient times took place, at Salamis in 480 BC. There, the Persians were decisively beaten by the Greek navy.

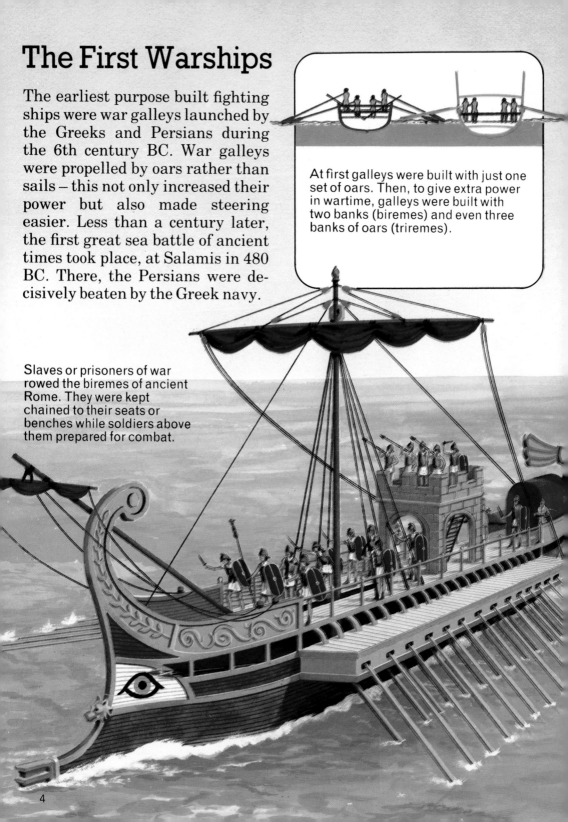

At first galleys were built with just one set of oars. Then, to give extra power in wartime, galleys were built with two banks (biremes) and even three banks of oars (triremes).

Slaves or prisoners of war rowed the biremes of ancient Rome. They were kept chained to their seats or benches while soldiers above them prepared for combat.

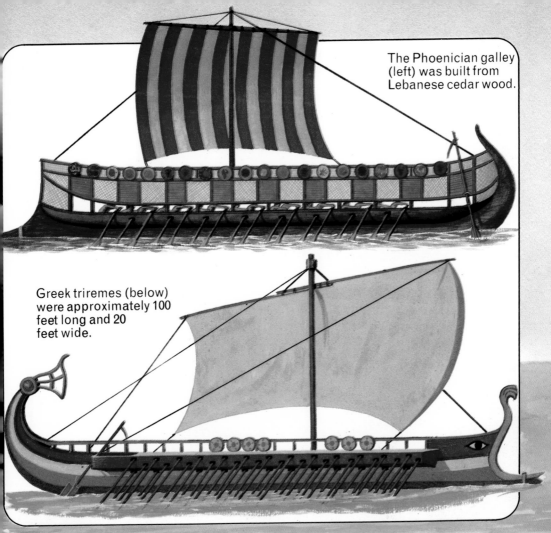

The Phoenician galley (left) was built from Lebanese cedar wood.

Greek triremes (below) were approximately 100 feet long and 20 feet wide.

The prow of a Roman war galley, with its eye and specially constructed battering ram bow.

War galleys were long, narrow and fast. Their bows were shaped to form a battering ram, and eyes were painted on their prows to "see" the enemies' ships. Propelled by their rowers' strength, they launched themselves at their enemies – like a spear or lance – and rammed them. When the enemy vessels were crippled, soldiers from the galleys leapt aboard them and fought, just as they did on land.

The Norsemen

During the late 8th century, the Vikings, or Norsemen, sailed from tree-lined Danish shores and the inlets of Scandinavian fiords to launch a series of sea raids along the coast of Western Europe. Their strong, sturdily built, shallow longboats were constructed of 2-inch thick oak planks. This made the vessels well able to withstand the stormy North Sea. Measuring between 70 and 80 feet long, Viking longboats had a central mast, a rising prow and stern, and a great many oars. The Vikings sailed around the coasts and rivers of Europe, terrorizing the towns and villages, often taking their victims by surprise. They attacked and looted monasteries, captured and carried off slaves, and forced entire regions to pay them protection money.

The routes the Viking longboats followed on their raids into Europe. These sturdy craft also reached Greenland and North America.

When William the Conqueror crossed the Channel from Normandy in 1066, he sailed in a vessel similar to those used by his Viking ancestors.

Like longboats, Norman ships were open, square sailed, had many oars and a curved shape. This style of warship continued well into the next two centuries. The Crusaders went to the Holy Land in *dromons* – popular warships of the Middle Ages. These were huge galleys, sometimes rowed by hundreds of people.

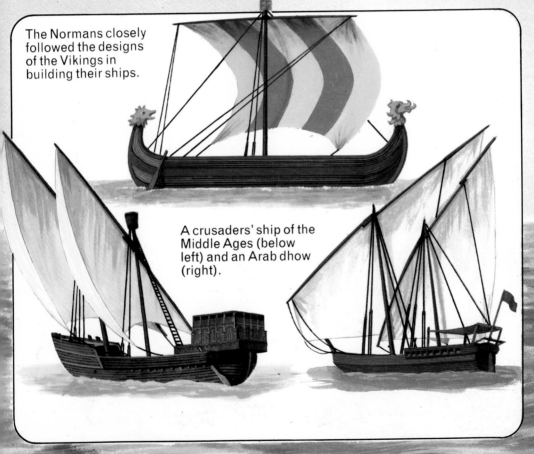

The Normans closely followed the designs of the Vikings in building their ships.

A crusaders' ship of the Middle Ages (below left) and an Arab dhow (right).

Galleons

By the 14th century, most fighting ships in Europe were too heavy to be propelled by oars, so they relied entirely on sail. Some vessels had temporary platforms (known as "castles") added after they were built. These castles were useful for launching attacks on other ships. Missiles could be thrown from the topcastle, which was fitted on the masthead. Alternatively, archers could stand on them or guns could be fitted to them.

Galleons were introduced in the 16th century during Henry VIII's reign. These huge, lumbering warships stood high in the water. They had several decks and were fitted with many guns. Galleons formed the bulk of the Spanish Armada which was defeated by the English in 1587.

Pirates began attacking ships in ancient times. In their search for gold and other treasures they brought terror to the high seas. The Barbary pirates of the Mediterranean menaced shipping for 300 years until the French occupied Algiers in 1830, ending piracy and making the Mediterranean safe for shipping.

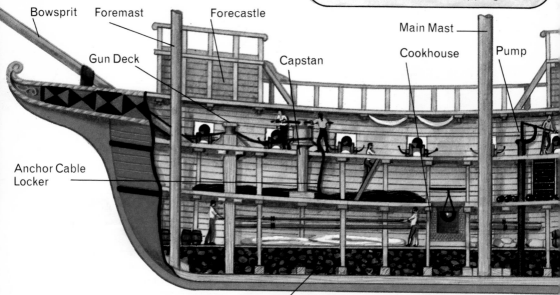

Bowsprit   Foremast   Forecastle   Main Mast   Gun Deck   Capstan   Cookhouse   Pump   Anchor Cable Locker   Ballast

Square sails were set
on the foremast and
main mast of a
galleon, with a lateen
sail on the mizzen
mast.

A cutaway illustration of a galleon,
showing the uses to which its decks
were put.

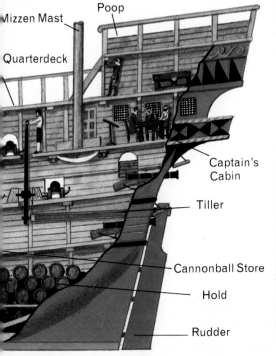

Mizzen Mast

Quarterdeck

Poop

Captain's
Cabin

Tiller

Cannonball Store

Hold

Rudder

The carrack (top) appeared during
the 15th century. It was used as a
merchant trader. The caravel (above)
was based on a Moorish design.
Portuguese explorers sailed down the
coast of Africa in ships like this.

Trafalgar

On October 21, 1805, ships of the British Royal Navy sighted Napoleon's French and Spanish fleets off Cape Trafalgar in the south of Spain. Napoleon was attempting yet again to take control of the seas from the British.

To prevent this, the Royal Navy's Commander in Chief, Lord Nelson, had invented a revolutionary tactic. He ordered the British ships to attack in two columns at right angles to the enemy. Nelson's plan worked – the British Navy won a complete victory though many sailors were killed or injured. The dead included Lord Nelson, who was fatally wounded on his ship.

Conditions on the gun decks below were made horrible by the thunder of cannon, the crashing recoil and the blinding, acrid smoke. The noise of the guns was so great that many seamen lost their hearing forever.

Half an hour after the battle of Trafalgar began, Nelson was fatally wounded by a French sharpshooter as he stood on the deck of HMS *Victory*. His last words were, "Thank God I have done my duty".

Iron and Steam

For thousands of years the world's fighting ships were powered by either the wind or oars. Then, with the invention of steam engines in the mid-1800s, ships with both sails and screw propellers appeared. As steam-driven ships could propel heavier vessels whatever the weather, armor-plating for warships soon followed.

The first ever battle between the so-called "ironclads" (shown below) was between the Confederate *Merrimack* and the Union *Monitor,* dubbed "a cheese-box on a raft". It took place in Hampton Roads, Virginia on March 9, 1862, during the Civil War. Thousands of people stood on the shore to watch the battle. In the event, neither ship's guns could damage the other, and the battle was a draw.

The Turtle was the first submarine used in war. In 1776, during the American Revolution, it was used in an attempt to blow up a British warship in New York harbor.

The *Gloire*, launched in 1860 at Toulon, France, was the world's first armored battleship. Its wooden hull was "clad" with an iron "belt" 4½ inches thick which extended from 6 feet below the water-line to the deck. The *Gloire* had a steam-powered screw in addition to its sails for power, and displaced about 560 tons. However, its 36 guns were too weak to make the *Gloire* a successful warship, and it was also not very seaworthy. Its sister ship, the *Normandie*, was the first armored ship to cross the Atlantic (1862).

Battleships

In World War I (1914-1918) the Allies and Germany both had very strong navies. Their chief warships were "dreadnoughts" – new, fast, heavily armored battleships with all their main guns about the same size (at least 11 inches, or 28 cm).

Many people expected a decisive battle between the two enemy fleets. In fact they only met once at Jutland in the North Sea in 1916. As a result of that bitter engagement, neither fleet ever again felt confident enough to put to sea. In the end, submarines, mines and torpedoes all proved more important than the massive, glamorous surface ships.

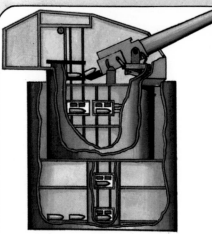

Britain's big naval guns of World War I were slightly larger than those of Germany. But German barrels lasted longer. Either side could hit a moving target at over 8-mile range. Here we see the shell-delivery system to a turret, which ensured that a hit on the turret would not explode the ship's magazine.

Submarines were virtually untried weapons in 1914. Torpedoes, too – and especially British ones – were also quite unreliable. Nonetheless, whereas most of Britain's underwater navy was simply used to patrol the coastline, the Germans boldly sent their U-boats (submarines) far out to sea. Vessels like the one below sank thousands of merchant vessels as well as numerous warships. There were even times when, despite the convoy system, U-boats almost succeeded in cutting all supply routes to Britain. Had they achieved this, Britain would almost certainly have been forced to surrender the war.

HMS *Queen Elizabeth,* a super-dreadnought

König, a German dreadnought

HMAS *Sydney,* a 5400-ton cruiser

La Gloire, a French armored cruiser

HMS *Furious,* the first "flat-top"

In 1914 – just a century after Trafalgar and 50 years after the first-ever ironclads – monsters like the 20,000-ton HMS *Dreadnought* (below) seemed like the last word in seapower. With a speed of 22 knots and 10 big guns, it certainly seemed invincible. But by 1919 the advent of air power and submarines had already begun to sound the death knell of floating fortresses like this one.

Battle of the Atlantic

In 1939 the German navy had several big warships (see right), but its greatest strength was its fleet of oceangoing U-boats. So, despite some sea battles between surface ships in the Atlantic and Mediterranean – such as the Battle of Matapan (1941), and the sinking of the *Bismarck* and HMS *Hood* (1941) – the main sea war in the West was the so-called Battle of the Atlantic.

This was the bitter struggle for Britain's Atlantic sea lanes, fought between "wolf-packs" of U-boats and convoys of Allied merchant ships under naval escort. After suffering terrible losses, the Allies finally gained the upper hand by 1943 with the aid of "asdic" (sonar) and air cover.

British coastal patrol submarine

German ocean-going *Unterseeboot* (U-boat)

Bismarck, the biggest battleship of its day at 50,000 tons

HMS *Illustrious*, a 23,000-ton carrier with room for 36 planes

HMS *Hood*, a 44,600-ton battleship

Scharnhorst, a 32,000-ton battle cruiser in dock for most of World War II

Prinz Eugen, a German heavy cruiser

Vittorio Venito, an Italian battleship

Midget submarines played a small but spectacular part in World War II. The British "human torpedo" was used to attack the *Tirpitz* in Norway in 1942 and – more successfully – several Italian warships later in the war.

The *Admiral Graf Spee* was an outstanding German "pocket battleship". It had the speed (26 knots) to outrun anything that could outgun it, and the guns to destroy anything it couldn't outrun. But after sinking several Allied merchant ships in the southern oceans, it was briefly engaged by three enemy cruisers on December 13, 1939. Hardly damaged, it turned tail and hid in the neutral estuary of the River Plate, in Uruguay. There the confused captain scuttled his ship and then committed suicide.

The heart of "Force H", a balanced British naval attack force comprising the cruiser HMS *Sheffield* (background), the carrier HMS *Ark Royal* (right) and the battleship HMS *Renown* (below).

17

War in the Pacific

The Pacific War began on December 7, 1941, when aircraft from a Japanese "carrier strike force" attacked U.S. warships at Pearl Harbor, Hawaii. For the next 3½ years the armies of both sides fought savagely on land while rival navies and air forces vied for control of the sea and air.

Aircraft carriers were vital to this struggle, backed up by other warships, from battleships to torpedo boats. At the Battles of the Coral Sea and Midway in 1942, the back of Japan's powerful carrier fleet was broken. From then on, it was only a matter of time before Japan was defeated.

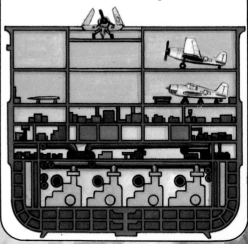

This cross-section of a U.S. Essex-class carrier from the lift looking aft shows clearly the mass of armor-plating along and below the waterline and on the flight deck, as well as the carefully shielded oil and fuel tanks around the bilges.

Displacing 27,100 tons and able to carry 100 aircraft at over 32 knots, Essex-class carriers were the backbone of the Allies' fast task forces (including other surface warships, submarines, troop transports and tankers) in the island-hopping Pacific War.

Above: The 64,170-ton Japanese *Yamato* – probably the greatest battleship of all time and heavily armed and armored. It entered service in 1945. On April 7, 1945, it was lost to the bombs, guns and torpedoes of 386 U.S. carrier aircraft.

Below: USS *Indianapolis,* a heavy cruiser that could pack almost the same punch as a battleship.

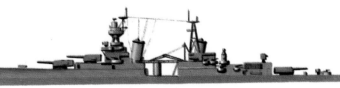

Below: A Porpoise class submarine, a type that sank hundreds of Japanese ships.

USS *Iowa,* a fast (28-knot) U.S. battleship with a main armament of nine guns and a crew of 2500. It served with success in the Pacific, and is shown here under dive-bombing attack from a Japanese Zero fighter.

The Modern Navy

Nuclear-powered submarines are now the capital ships of the world's leading navies. They carry computer-controlled nuclear missiles and stay submerged for months.

To track and if necessary destroy these underwater prowlers, the superpowers now use specialized "hunter-killer" submarines as well as fast, missile-armed surface ships, especially frigates.

Guns are almost redundant in this new type of warfare. Instead, modern warships carry helicopters, computers, radar and other electronic tracking and weapons systems. Meanwhile, aircraft carriers still have a big part to play. The USA successfully used its huge fleet carriers as "floating airfields" during the Vietnam War.

A modern British anti-submarine (AS) frigate, HMS *Gurkha*.

Left: A Westland Lynx AS helicopter.

Above: The huge (80,000-ton) U.S. nuclear-powered carrier USS *Enterprise*, shown here launching a Sea Harrier V/STOL strike aircraft.

Since the advent of orbiting satellites, helicopters, and mid-air refueling, naval and air warfare have become closely connected.

Missile-armed helicopters carrying sonar "dips" are well-suited to "hunter-killer" duties against submarines. Special "helicopter carriers" have been built to be their floating bases. Also, smaller carriers equipped with both helicopters and V/STOL aircraft are now entering service. They can be used to launch strikes against land targets, surface ships, or submarines. In the future, though, no fighting ships will be safe without overall control of their airspace.

Below: A Sikorsky Sea King AS helicopter seen dangling its sonar "dip" which picks up the sound of submarines.

Above: An RAF Nimrod patrol and reconnaissance aircraft – equipped to track and destroy submarines.

Below: Russia's Yankee-class missile-armed submarine.

Below: A French nuclear submarine, Redoutable.

Below: HMS Resolution, one of Britain's fleet of big Polaris submarines.

Since they began to enter service in the 1960s, nuclear-powered submarines like this one have been the capital ships of Western navies. They carry 16 Polaris missiles armed with nuclear warheads. Each has a pre-set target in Russia and together with air-launched weapons they make up the main strategic weapons force. With two complete crews – one ashore and one at sea – these mysterious vessels can stay in non-stop service year after year. And by diving deep and recycling their air they can remain submerged and possibly even undetected for months at a time.

21

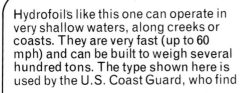

Hydrofoils like this one can operate in very shallow waters, along creeks or coasts. They are very fast (up to 60 mph) and can be built to weigh several hundred tons. The type shown here is used by the U.S. Coast Guard, who find it very useful for patrolling such areas as the bayous of the Mississippi delta and Florida's Everglades swamps. In such theaters, the enemies are not usually Russian or Cuban commandoes, but most likely people trying to smuggle drugs into the country from the Caribbean or South America. However, the future wartime uses of such vessels are obvious.

Special Ships

During the Korean War of 1950-1953, the use of special craft, such as the hovercraft shown on the right, was merely experimental. Such vessels have since become a standard part of all the world's major military forces.

Riding on a cushion of air over mud flats or water, these military hovercraft can travel at speeds of up to 50 mph.

Glossary

Conning Tower The superstructure of a submarine.

Flight Deck The part of an aircraft carrier from which planes take off and land.

Forecastle or **Fo'c'sle** Raised deck in the bows.

Lateen A triangular sail running fore-and-aft and often used on the mizzen mast of sailing ships to aid steering.

Magazine The parts of a ship used to store ammunition.

Mizzen The mast at the stern of a ship, often carrying a lateen sail.

Poop A raised deck at the stern.

Port Left hand side of a ship (looking forward).

Quarterdeck The upper deck running from the stern to the main mast. Often the part of the deck reserved for officers.

Rigging The ropes used to support masts, and to control sails.

Rudder Flat blade fixed to the stern which is turned to steer a ship.

Sonar Ultrasonic Depth-sounding equipment used to record the depth of the sea or to detect submarines or other underwater objects. It is also known as "asdic" and operates on the same principles as radar.

Starboard Right hand side of a ship (looking forward).

Superstructure The parts of a ship built on above the main deck.

V/STOL Vertical or short take off and landing aircraft like the Sea Harrier (see page 20), which do not require the long runways used by other planes and which are therefore suitable for aircraft carriers.

Index